Geo. E. (George Everett) Foster

Reminiscences of travel in Cherokee Lands

Geo. E. (George Everett) Foster

Reminiscences of travel in Cherokee Lands

ISBN/EAN: 9783337190972

Printed in Europe, USA, Canada, Australia, Japan

Cover: Foto ©Andreas Hilbeck / pixelio.de

More available books at **www.hansebooks.com**

REMINISCENCES

OF

TRAVEL IN

CHEROKEE LANDS.

AN ADDRESS

DELIVERED BEFORE THE LADIES' MISSIONARY
SOCIETY OF THE ITHACA, N. Y., CON-
GREGATIONAL CHURCH, 1898.

———

BY GEO. E. FOSTER.

———

ITHACA, N. Y.
DEMOCRAT PRESS,
1899.

PROLOGUE.

———

As I was the first white man to write a book devoted to showing the rise of the Cherokee Nation from barbarism to a comparatively high state of civilization through the inspiration and genius of Se-quo-yah, their great schoolmaster, prophet and chief, the Cherokee Senate passed a resolution of thanks for my interest in trying to prove to the too incredulous and willingly misled American people, that there could be something great and even good in the American Indian, and several letters were forwarded to me from the Cherokee people requesting that I should visit them in their homes and accept their hospitalities as a Nation.

These invitations were accepted for some time in the future, but I must confess that my departure for the Cherokee capitol was hastened somewhat by the heartiness of a renewal in the handwriting of Hon. William P. Boudinot, who was then Executive Secretary of the Cherokee Nation and whose father was the first Cherokee editor.

"We do not again ask you to visit us," he wrote, "as you have already consented to do so, Providence willing, but we expect you pursuant to understanding. Only give us a little time, please, not to give us a chance to brush up for any report that you may wish to make, but, so that we can make your visit as pleasant as is possible on your own account."

The warmness of the invitation touched a responsive chord in my heart, and I would go at once, not even waiting for the little notice beforehand. And so I went. It did not take me long to get ready, for had I not been educated to the idea that there was only a vast wilderness before me into which only an elephant would carry a trunk.

But before my return I learned a lesson. I learned the possibilities of raising a people from darkness into light. I returned more ready than ever, to take off my hat and bow

with reverence to the memory of good Queen
Isabella, that queen, who had tenderest con-
cern for the humane and mild usage of
Indians presided over by her subjects in this
country, and those laudable sentiments were
adopted into the laws of Spain so far as they
related to America, and served as the introduction to the regulations contained under
the title "Good Government of Indians."
I returned also feeling more than ever like
extolling the name of Ferdinand, who op-
posed all Dominicans, who believed it a waste
of time to communicate the sublime truths of
religion to Indians until their spirits were
broken and their faculties impaired by oppres-
sion, and who for religion's sake favored the
barbarous treatment to the untutored children
of the forests. And, I would again bow my
head reverently to Anne, the English queen,
whose reign was so noted for its magnificence;
who notwithstanding all her love of splendor,
took time and pains to, and did win the love
of the combined Iroquois nations, and so won
the hearts of the chiefs that they wept when
they heard of her death, and long they remembered the kindness that she showed to those

Indians residing on the vast tract of country governed by her. Indeed, on my return from the Nation Cherokee, I felt prouder than ever, that on the pages of American history stands the name of Wm. Penn, an honest man in dealing with all Indians.

Let memory forever cherish the name of Helen Hunt Jackson, whose published works have done so much to create in the hearts of the American people a spirit leading to more just treatment of an oppressed race. and who by her arraignment of land-grabbers, politicians and inhuman government officials, has placed the cause of much heralded "Indian barbarities," just where it belongs, viz., in the barbarity, greed and inhumanity of unworthy pale-faces of an alleged civilized people. Let the names of Herbert Welsh and Mrs. Quinton, those organizers of societies to oppose unjust legislation and to preserve the rights of the red men of today, be ever treasured among those already emblazoned on the tablets of enduring memory as true benefactors of the human race.

THROUGH

CHEROKEE LANDS.

I.

You are invited to take a journey with me to the Cherokee Nation, via St. Louis, and while our train is making the first part of our trip, we will, if you please, use that time in getting acquainted with the Cherokee Indians whom we are about to visit,—Who are they? Whence came they? How came they in the land where they now reside?

The Cherokees have been styled the "Mountaineers of Aboriginal America," but there were two branches, called the "Upper" and "Lower" Cherokees, their name having sole reference to the portion of country in which they lived.

Not long after America was discovered by

the white men, a navigator representing a monarch of the British Isles sailed along the coast
opposite the lands which had been discovered
centuries before by the Indian owners of the
country.   This navigator never set foot upon
the shore at all ; he simply looked upon the
land and claimed it for Great Britain by right
of discovery, and from that time on the trou-
bles of the Cherokee Indians began.   For it
is a fact, that very long before any white man
visited the shores of North America to the
southward and among the mountains of Vir-
ginia, and in that territory called South and
North Carolina. Georgia and Tennessee, there
dwelt several tribes of Indians, having customs and laws of their own ; they were little
nations ; and of these little nationalities, the
Cherokees were accounted one.   The Cherokees had held possession of the land so long
that they could not tell when first found by
the white men whether they owned the country by right of discovery or by conquest.

But in 1732 a monarch of several Isles on
the eastern coast of the Atlantic Ocean, under
the style and name of George II., King of
Great Britain and Ireland, affected to grant a

great tract of country belonging to Indians between the 26th and 38th parallel of North Latitude, the object being, so records tell us, to provide a home for the poor of Great Britain and Ireland; it was proposed for this purpose to raise a fund, which should be expended in the conveyance of indigent emigrants to that part of America free of expense. The plan was countenanced by "humane and opulent men," and on June 9th, 1732, King George II. granted to these Britain and Ireland paupers the land of several sovereign Indian nations.

The lower Indians, who were lower in intellect than the upper Cherokees who dwelt among the mountains, insisted that the Cherokees originally came out of a hole in the ground, but as they found no hole in the territory that they then possessed, they thought it must have been located west of a big river which was the Mississippi. They had a tradition that they came over the river on a grapevine bridge.*

---

*Now, by way of parenthesis let me say, that a grapevine is a great institution in the Indian country. The children use them for swings; the In-

I used to think that the lower Cherokees' belief that they first sprung from a hole in the ground was very stupid on their part. But having been taught no other way, as Indians always do, they took Nature as a text book. They would go out in the morning, and looking on the ground, where there had been nothing visible the night before, would behold scores of little ant-hills from which thousands of little ants were swarming, and it was from them they obtained the idea that by some

---

dian women use them for clothes lines ; and they are often used as a bridge. Firstly, just think of an Indian girl walking over a wide stream on a grapevine, which had a diameter of less than four inches. And then secondly, just think of a white man attempting to walk over that same vine. I tried it once when a little Cherokee girl took me out walking. She went over as easy as you would walk up a city's widest and best sidewalk ; but when I tried it, I, who went out there into the woods as a visitor from undoubted civilization,— well, if I must admit it, I will ; the little barbarian just laughed, and I found it very mortifying for a male representative of civilization to be laughed at by an Indian young lady just because he could not walk over a grapevine bridge as quickly and gracefully and safely as she could.

such outpouring, their forefathers had been allowed by the Great Spirit to people the land.

But the upper Cherokees, those that in history have been styled the "Mountaineers of Aboriginal America," had a higher idea of their origin. It is in substance as follows :

*In the time Nu-ta-te-qua, or the first new moon of Autumn, U-ha-li-te-qua, the great-great, or the head of all power, great beyond expression, having also A-ta-no-ti and U-sqa-hu-la, two other beings of like sentiment and action, in the Great Council House above the gilt-edged clouds beyond the mountains, sat on three seats, which were covered with the purest white fur, and surrounded with trusty spirits. These three were the proprietors of all things that then were, for all that then was by them had been constructed. They were indeed the great-great, for when U-ha-li-te-qua, A-ta-no-ti and U-sqa-hu-la said "live," life came ; when they said "die" death followed.

But at this time, they were discussing where to fix their permanent abode and they concluded to first finish their work of creation.

---

*A Buttrick Antiquity.

The first firmament which they created was somewhat higher than a mountain, but it proved too narrow and too warm and not high enough to behold all their subjects. Then U-ha-li-te-qua, A-ta-no-ti and U-sqa-hu-la built a second firmament that also proved too small and warm, but as it proved more comfortable than the first, they decided to keep on building firmaments until they should find one just right. They did so, and in the seventh they decided to make their home. Then U-ha-li-te-qua, A-ta-no-ti and U-sqa-hu-la became absorbed into one being as they had been before in sentiment and action.

This being was called Ye-ho-wa.

The early Cherokees believed him to be both man and Spirit, a very glorious being, whose name was never to be spoken in common talk. To him bowing toward the East they addressed their prayers, just before the rising sun.

Within the first firmament, Ye-ho-wa created the earth and in it he made a beautiful garden. And it came to pass that Ye-ho-wa and his son—for the earliest Cherokees say he had a son—decided to people the earth, and the time was Nu-ta-te-qua or Autumn, when the fruits were all ripe.

Then Ye-ho-wa sent his son to manage the affairs of earth, and he descended to the garden and made two images out of clay, and when he had completed them, his father, Ye-ho-wa, breathed into the bodies, a soul, heart and inwards, and one became a male and the other a female. The clay of which they were made was red; hence this man and woman were the progenitors of the red race.

It seems to have been a fact that the Indians gave what we may call a local color to their descriptions of their hells. I never understood why the Southern Indian always punished the souls of their wicked dead with fires of burning pitch, until I visited their old stamping grounds, the turpentine forests of the South. Nothing earthly is much hotter than burning pitch. I never understood why the mountain Cherokees so often had the accursed souls of their dead transfixed on sharp stakes, in dark and deep abysses, until I myself stood beside those deep mountain crevices and looked tremblingly over on the uplifting sharp spines of broken trees, which were reaching up to pierce through any victim that might chance to fall into the gulf below.

I have wondered sometimes how it came to pass that the Indians have a tradition of a hell in which the victims are tormented by blades of sharpened steel. I have thought, but do not know, that this tradition is not older than the time when white men began to drive by the point of the bayonet the Indians from their homes that they loved so well and the graves of their fathers.

When first discovered by the white men, the Cherokees were a religious people, though they were not religious according to white men's lights, but were religious notwithstanding. They were not idolaters, for I have never found a proven statement that they worshipped idols. They had a story of the Genesis not unlike that of the white men's Bible. This, I think can be traced to the influence of the Spaniard, Cabeca. He taught the Southern Indians the story of the Genesis, and it was handed down by the story-tellers of various tribes.

Wassi was he who warned the Cherokees

of a coming flood; he was a prophet who foretold events. The enchanted mountain in Union County, Georgia, was the Ararat of the Cherokees. Santa Rosa Mountain was the Ararat of the Pimas, which was another tribe in the South. The eagle warned the Pimas' prophet of the approaching flood and advised him to prepare for it. The warning came three times, and suddenly, the winds arose and the rain descended in torrents; the thunder and lightning were terrific, and darkness covered the world. Everything on earth was destroyed, and all Pimas perished except one chief, "So Ho," a good and brave Indian, who was saved by special interposition of the Great Spirit. In his canoe, surrounded by his family and animals, he weathered the storm and, when the waters subsided, he found himself on the mountain of Santa Rosa. The Cherokee Noah escaped with various animals and in a canoe drawn by a bevy of very beautiful swans he at last landed on the enchanted mountain in Georgia.*

---

*The Choctaws were neighbors of the Cherokees and their tradition of the flood was as follows: "At a very remote period, there was a great deluge,

Gladly would we linger on the beautiful traditions of the Cherokees, but time forbids.

---

which spread over the whole earth. It was preceded by a preternatural darkness, the people went to sleep at the commencement of this darkness as usual, and after sleeping the usual time they awoke and found it still dark. They awoke again and found it still dark. Again they slept, and awoke and darkness was on the face of the earth. This excited alarm. The darkness was so great, that neighbors could have no intercourse with each other except by torch light. After some time they discovered, as they thought, the dawning of the day in the east. This occasioned great joy, and they went from house to house to congratulate each other on the return of light. But they were soon undeceived; for what they had supposed to be light proved to be a great body of water, like the sea, which, coming with great velocity, swept away all before it. Some few, who were on more elevated situations succeeded in making rafts and getting upon them, but the beavers gnawed off the bark, by which the logs of the raft were tied together, and thus, after having their hopes raised by escaping the destruction which was all around them, they were plunged into the water and irretrievably lost. One raft, however, made of reeds, escaped the ravages of the beavers, and out-rode the storm, and all who were on it were saved; but the number is not known.

I have already spoken of the part an eagle took in the foretelling events, which calls to mind the first known political convention between the Cherokees and the English people.

It was in one of the mother towns in 1730, that the Cherokees made their first alliance with the English.   It was brought about by one Alexander Cumming, who had traveled extensively among the Southern Indians. Just how he won over the Indians to his project is misty history, but on the day when the Cherokees swore allegiance to Great Britain, there was a mighty gathering of Cherokees in one of the mother towns, and at last they seated Sir Alexander Cumming on a stump that was well covered with fur, and then, with the same number of eagles' tails as there are stripes today on the American flag, they began to stroke Sir Alexander, and their singers sang about him from morning to night, when all the warriors of the Cherokees bowed on their knees and declared themselves to be dutiful subjects of King George, and called upon all that was terrible and that they might become as no people, if they in any way violated their promise of obedience.

Now this marching, and this stroking Sir Alexander Cumming with those thirteen eagles' tails, I am convinced was the first appearance of the American eagle in politics in America, notwithstanding the historians say, that it was not in 1730, but in 1785, that the American eagle became our national emblem.

II

With the turning of this leaf, a hundred and
six years have passed away since the Cherokees made their first alliance with the English.
Much has happened: England has now no
part in American politics. The Cherokees
have been visited by the missionaries. God
has raised up from one of their number an
earthly Saviour, Se-quo-yah. He had invented
the most wonderful alphabet that this world
has known. The Bible had been translated
into it. The Cherokees had good homes.
schools and churches. The work of missionaries had truly blest. By their state of civilization the Cherokees were styled a nation, and
our good old friend, Rev. Samuel A. Worcester, whom I told you about last year. was one
of their number. Gold had been found in
Cherokee lands, and the tribe was in the way
of the ever encroaching white men,—white

men, who from the first settlement of America, have seen no place for red-men, the rightful owners of the soil, but have willingly given homes to the often criminal emigrants of foreign lands. By laws passed the Indians were forbidden to dig for gold on their own land and then that terrible law was decreed by the white men that no Indian, or descendant of an Indian, residing within the Cherokee nation should be deemed a competent witness to any suit in any court where a white man was a defendant. This is only one specimen of the laws passed to throw the Indians into the greatest confusion in order that they might be more easily overcome, destroyed or forced from the land of their nativity.

Now I wish right here to sum up in six propositions, what might make an equal number of long chapters.

First ; We have shown that the Cherokees were a happy people, who were living on the lands which seemingly had been deeded to them by Almighty God, and they were becoming civilized.

Second ; Feeling the germs of civilization sprouting in their breasts, they paralyzed the white men by deciding to organize a government of their own on a civilized plan.

Third ; The white men who had appropriated the Indian lands made it a law, that no separate nation could be allowed to be formed within the boundaries of the State.

Fourth ; The white men drew a state line around the budding Cherokee Nation.

Fifth ; They forbid the Indians from digging gold on their own lands. thus making it of little value to them.

Sixth ; Then they made that infamous law just quoted forbidding Indians from being witnesses or complainants in any court where a white man was a defendant, and then having made their land of little value to them ; and having made their hope of home-government impossible and having made laws so cruel that they could not live under them. what next did the white men of a so-called christian civilization do ?   I will tell you what they did. They bribed some of the Cherokees to barter their country for gold. and the United States sanctioned the unlawful sale by the minority in spite of a most pathetic appeal of the majority.*   They then in exchange gave to the

---

*The following is the text of this appeal, which, probably designedly, is left out of modern histories :

"By the stipulation of this instrument, (the treaty of New Echota [1836]), we are despoiled of our private possessions ; we are stripped of every attribute of freedom and eligibility for legal defense. Our property may be plundered before our eyes. Violence may be committed upon our persons ; even our lives may be taken away and there are none to regard our complaint. We are denationalized ! We are disfranchised ! We are deprived of membership with human family ! We have neither land nor home nor resting place to call our own, and this is effected by the provisions of a compact, which assumes the venerated, the sacred appellation of "treaty." We are overwhelmed ! Our hearts are sickened ! Our utterance is paralyzed, when we reflect on the condition in which we are placed by unprincipled men, who have managed their stratagems with such dexterity as to impose on the Government of the United States, in the face of our earnest, solemn and re-iterated protestations. This instrument in question is not the act of our Nation. We are not parties to its covenants. It has not received the sanction of our people. The makers of it sustain no office or appointment in our Nation under the designation of chiefs, headsmen or any title by

Indians a tract of land which the Government supposed was worthless, and believed it was so far outside of creation that the Cherokee would be forever removed from the path of the white man. And right here I wish to say, that that dear Christian missionary, Rev. Samuel A. Worcester, whom I told you about one

---

which they hold or could acquire authority to assume the reins of government, and to make, bargain and sale of our common country. We are indeed an afflicted people! Our spirits are subdued! Despair has well nigh seized our energies! But we speak to the representatives of a Christian country, the friends of justice, the patrons of the oppressed, and our prospects brighten as we indulge the thought that on your sentence our fate is suspended. Prosperity or desolation depends upon your word. To you therefore we look! Before your august assembly we present ourselves in the attributes of depreciation, and of entreaty. On your kindness, on your judgment, on your humanity, on your compassion, on your benevolence we rest our hopes. To you we address our reiterated prayers. Spare our people! Spare the wreck of our prosperity! Let not our deserted homes become the monuments of desolation. We suppress the agonies which wring our hearts, when we look at our wives, our children and our venerable sires. We restrain our forebodings of anguish

year ago, was with other missionaries thrown
into prison where they were kept a long time
because they rightfully stood by the Cherokees in their time of trouble.

Well, you say, "what next?"   I will tell you
what happened next.   Having made the illegal
trade they ordered the Indians to leave the
homes they had builded and go to the far off
and untried wilderness.*   But many refused

---

and distress, of misery and devastation and death
which must be the attendance on the execution of
this ruinous compact."

Such an appeal as that ought to have melted a
heart of stone.   But how was it met by the United
States?   On Nov. 3, 1836, the Secretary of the War
Department answered these anxious Cherokees as
follows :

"I am instructed by the President of the United
States to say that no delegation that may be sent
to Washington with a view of obtaining new terms,
or a modification of the existing treaty, will be received or recognized, nor will any intercourse be
held with them directly or indirectly or in
writings."

*The author has before him a personal letter
written from one connected with a missionary station in the old Cherokee county.   Under date of
June, 1838, he wrote : "That time specified in the
fraudulent treaty for the removal of the Cherokees

to go, and then one spring morning in 1838 there came from all sides of the old Cherokee land except the westward the tramp, tramp, tramp of United States troops, and at the point of the bayonet sixteen thousand Chero-

---

and the memorials from various parts of the United States presented to Congress have been disregarded, and the only future seems to be they must now be forced from their peaceful homes and firesides to a land where there is not a sufficient scope for such a company. Indeed were you here and did you know the true facts, you nor any other man who is not destitute of human feelings could refrain from weeping for the afflicted hosts. There is now a large military force in the country, commanded by Gen. Scott, for the purpose of collecting the Cherokees and transporting them to the west. Indeed they have already commenced this wicked act, while at the same time the principal chief of the Nation, and others with him, are at the seat of Government praying Congress to desist from such fraudulent measures, but I fear to no purpose, for some have already been taken from their houses, leaving all their property to the rule of their enemies, and thus like sheep to some place of embarkation. O, the awful guilt and stain on our American Government. The society of the Cherokees is far preferable to that of most of those who have come into this country to settle.

kee Indians were gathered into four great herds, like so many cattle. Then came the long and terrible march across the country and in the six months' time, four thousand of the forced emigration died of sickness caused by hardships and broken hearts.

Perhaps you remember about the Indian woman in that lowly cabin which I told you about one year ago?* I mean her, who in the rude sticks that held up the decaying timbers of her hut was so happy and content that she could compare them to the more stately pillars of a council house; I mean her whose life was devoted to caring for others poorer than herself; I mean her who was the great aunt of the little Cherokee maiden whose dreams gave to the Cherokee people their first sacred hymn. Well as I sat in her lowly cabin, just as I told you about last year, I asked her if she remembered that terrible march across the country. "Yes, oh yes," she said, "I was weel young then, but I often wondered on the way why my people never ceased to weep."

---

*Story of the Cherokee Bible, page 40.

I think I hear some one say that the Christian Government of the United States would not use such means today to get the Indian lands.   But here we must differ in opinion.

III

Fifty years more pass and civilization reaches the land which in 1836 had been deeded to the Indians in exchange for the old Cherokee country. The white men wanted their land once more.

A few years ago when I was in the Cherokee Nation at a time when at Washington the orators were trying to convince the world that the Cherokees had no right to their western land, as a special favor the treasurer of the Cherokee Nation with the consent of the Chief opened the great safe in the Cherokee Council House. He took out a metallic tube, and having uncapped the same, he drew forth a parchment gaily trimmed with eagle feathers. It was the deed of their land as it was given by the United States Government. I read that deed. I saw the signature of the President of the United States and others in authority. It was as strong a deed as it was possible for the United States to give, and then in their joy at having at what they supposed to be the best of the bargain, and perhaps to make the deed more pleasing to the Cherokees, they trimmed the parchment with eagles' feathers.

Many of us have read how the Cherokees sold to the United States the famous Cherokee strip. We have read the Government reports of the amicable trade with the Indians ; even ministers of the Gospel have unwittingly thanked God in their pulpits that the question was settled in such a Christian manner. Was it?

How little the people in general know of the real meaning of many acts of Congress. It had turned out that the land deeded to the Indians was better than the white men thought when they traded it to the Cherokees prior to 1838. It turned out that it became an eyesore for the land-grabber, and the paid politicians. This territory had become very valuable to the Cherokees as they rented it to the white men for grazing purposes, and they received for rental the sum of over two hundred thousand dollars yearly, and with that money the Cherokees maintained their government, two colleges and over a hundred schools, asking no help from the United States. In fact the Cherokees were at last a prosperous people. There was much to say in their favor, and about the only thing, in the land-grabbers' minds, that could be said against them was that they owned the land and had a deed of it.

Of course the Cherokees saw the value of the property that gave them an income that supported their Government and schools and a surplus that they divided per capita every two years. Why should they sell the Cherokee strip? Yet they sold it. The only way the members of Congress saw to get the land was to make it worthless, and this they did so far as the Indians were concerned. And it was done in this way; a bill was one day sprung upon Congress, accompanied with seductive speeches to the effect that no Indian should be permitted to rent his land for grazing purposes. Shame be it to our country! It became a law that no Indian could rent the land he owned for grazing, and thus the land of many an Indian had for him no value. What next? The land-grabbing politician began to send delegations to treat with the Cherokees for the lands which were still valuable for the white men although they had been made so worthless to the Cherokee. These delegations endeavored to frighten the Indians by hinting that if they did not take the price offered, which was but a pittance of what these lands were worth to the white men, that the deed which the United States had executed might be found to be null and void, and that they consequently might lose their land and the offered money as well, and so, the Cherokees yielded. And this is how the land-grab was "amicably settled" by the Government of the United States.

My friends, a visitor to any fair city or land can see the good side, or the bad side, and so report; they can tell of our homes, our educational institutions and of our peaceful home life, or if they choose, they can report on slums, and people of low estate. I found that which was bad in the Indian Territory and I found much that was good. Which is the best way, when we speak of a people to make the bad prominent, or speak of the good and true of a people's struggle to elevate rather than a tendency to degrade themselves. I believe it is far more important if we work for God and civilization to show what mission work has done for humanity rather than to show what it has not accomplished.

IV.

Having passed over the trail of death leading from the old Cherokee Nation to the new,
we pass into the Indian Territory as it is
today. Soon we are at the banks of a river,
or where three rivers flow side by side in a
single channel, the waters of the one muddy,
the other blue, and the third red. The waters
flow on side by side unmingled as far as the
eye can reach. Two Indians take us over the
ferry and we are indeed in the Indian country. We climb into a wagon of doubtful form,
and by mule power* we will journey on.

*One day while riding behind a pair of what
seemed to be particularly vicious mules, I noted
the peculiar ball of hair at the extremity of their
tails. Naturally I asked the why of it. "Mules
will kick," said the Creek Indian driver, "until
we teach them not to. We first tie a stone attached
to a rope to their tails, and let them kick. They
naturally look around to see what they have hit,

Beautiful indeed were the flowers on either side, and butterflies of gorgeous colors and in great numbers flitted in the glorious sunshine. A butterfly of unusually bright dress for some time flitted by our carriage. The Indian driver looked joyfully at it for a while and then asked me if I had ever heard the legend of the sun's daughter. I replied in the negative. "It is an old tradition among us," he said, "that in the beginning, a great number of beings were employed in constructing the sun, which planet was made first. It was the intention of the Great Spirit, that men should live always, but the sun having surveyed the land, and finding an insufficiency for their support, changed the design, and arranged that all men should die. The daughter of the sun was the first to suffer under the law, as

---

and when they see the suspended stone they kick again ; they of course hit the stone and again look back, and seeing it swing back and forth they continue to kick until they are sick of it. After that, we dress the mule's tail as you see, and that bunch of hair is a reminder to the mules as they look around, of their experience with the stone, and they never afterward kick so long as they are thus ornamented."

she was bitten by a serpent and died. There-upon, the sun decreed that men should live always. He then commissioned a few persons to seek the spirit of his daughter. which had taken the form of a beautiful butterfly, and to return it encased in a box. The search for the spirit was a long one, but, at last, the searchers found it hovering over a cluster of Cherokee roses. They started in pursuit, but her spirit coyly led them a long race through fields, dells and rocky fastnesses. but they wearied her out at last. and shut her in the box. But in their voyage home one of the party desired to see her again, and peeped into the box. She quickly escaped and became invisible to them. Immortality fled, and since then it has been decreed that all men must die."

V.

A Sabbath morn has dawned upon a charming, flower-decked prairie. All is quiet, peaceful, restful. The sunrise is such as would thrill an artist's soul and give inspiration for his finest work—and later, had there been a tree to mark by its shadow the time, it would have been half-past the hour of nine. What is it that I see speeding toward us far off over the prairie? What is that over there? What is that to the east; to the north and south? What there? What here? What yonder? They are Indian ponies, surely, and can it be?—On the back of each Indian pony sits an Indian maiden; picturesque indeed! Note their wide rimmed hats covering jetty locks and the red cloaks floating gracefully from their shoulders, as with wondrous speed the ponies pace the prairie. How soon they all pass us with nod and smile. Whence go they all ? Yonder we see a Mission Church, placed there by the earnest work of Ladies' Missionary Societies in the states, the result of combined efforts of just such societies as is this to which I speak tonight. What blessed work is accomplished by such societies as yours, my friends. To yon Mission Church those Indian ponies bear their precious burdens; with quiet bound the maidens dismount, leaving their steeds to the care of gallant Indian boys. You can well guess they had come from their far off homes to attend the Sunday School.

When we speak of "God's Acre" we associate the term with a cemetery. Let me tell you about an Indian "God's Acre." Way out in that wild country was a fertile plot of ground, well tilled and bearing fruit and vegetables of various kinds; it was cared for as well as our gardens in the states. It was tilled and cared for by Indian men and women far better than they worked their gardens at home. They call this "God's Acre" for right here each year they held a religious meeting of several days' duration in the Autumn. The fruit and vegetables were to feed the multitude who came, either out of curiosity or to worship. What a grand idea, my friends, to devote this land, and their labor, for the benefit of their people. How glad I was to find a so-called barbarian race making God's Acre a thing of life, even an avenue toward eternal life;—and yet it made me sad to think that God's Acre of the white men was so often only a graveyard. By this time, the Sunday School in the Mission Church must be over. We have had no prancing ponies to take us to the place of worship; if we had, we doubtless would have tumbled off, for we could hardly ride without saddle, and, these Indian maids sometimes do, without bridle. I saw one day an Indian woman riding to the public spring, and she carried a three year old child in her arms; when she reached the spring she bounded from the horse with the child in her arms; she kneeled down and drank as the horse quenched his thirst and then taking the great lusty boy in her arms, she sprang on the horse's back and rode away, perhaps as much annoyed at my apparent astonishment as I was at her surprising agility. Let us enter the mission church, for it is said that a full-blood Cherokee preacher is to address the audience. Let us test, if you please, the effectiveness of Indian gesture. We have all read about it. Will we be able to even guess what this Cherokee Indian is to talk about in his native tongue ? Yonder comes our Indian preacher; what a magnificent form; what a majestic tread. How devoutly he kneels and silently prays, and how musical his voice as he gives out the hymn. Do Cherokees sing? My friends, why do you not ask the same about the birds? The Cherokees are natural musicians. One evening I was invited down into a Cherokee parlor where there were twelve Indian youths and I, of course, was the thirteenth. A violin was on the table, which the first youth took up and played a tune, the next took it and played another, and the next and the next;—all drew the sweetest of music from that violin; it reached the tenth. The eleventh and the twelfth Indian played his tune and handed the violin to the thirteenth which was unlucky me, and I like the white woman of civilization had to decline because I had a cold. I tell you my friends, it is very mortifying to a civilized white man to go west to see so-called barbarians, and find that they can do civilization often better than he can. That night when that violin was passed to me as I looked for some way of escape; I would have given a ten dollar bill to have been able to have played a single strain of New England's old fashioned dancing tune of "Pop Goes the Weasel."

I remember reading somewhere of a time when the first missionaries among the Cherokees were much frightened at the approach of a big and reputed fierce chief of the Cherokees with a party of his braves. They did not know what to do, but they prayed silently and sang loudly as best they could, a beautiful hymn. The chief and his braves finally sat in a semicircle and looked entranced and so the missionaries kept on singing until the old chief rose up and came forward and struck his hand on his breast and said "me heart sing too." A concert by Indian young ladies was given in my honor while I was at the Cherokee Capitol and it was a fine one I assure you. I found many pianos and organs in that far off land.

VI

But I have wandered in my remarks far away from the mission chapel and our Indian preacher. I was speaking of his gestures. No matter in what position an Indian stands, he will make no mistake in his gesture when indicating the point of the compass. Many white orators make a gesture toward the west when speaking of the east, but an Indian makes no such mistake. If he points to the east he means the east, the rising sun, or something pertaining to the east. So I had in the beginning a clew to what this Cherokee had to say. As he pointed toward the east he shaded his eyes with his hand and so it was safe to guess, that what he saw to the eastward was light. Was it the light, fire, the golden sun, the hunter's moon, or, was it a silvery star? He could not mean fire, for as he spoke his eye and finger began to trace a

course from the horizon to the zenith. It
could not be the sun that he meant, for had it
been, he would have continued to shade his
eyes with his hand. It was not the hunter's
moon, for he crouched not his body in that
stealthy attitude of the Indian hunter. Then
he must mean a star, and, by the time I had
guessed it, the Indian preacher had traced its
orbit to a point directly overhead and there
his finger stopped. I remembered only two
Biblical stories in which any of the celestial
orbs stood still. The first was where Joshua
commanded the sun and moon to stand still,
but I have already told you that the preacher
had proved to me that that of which he spoke
was a star. At what other time did the star
stand still in the zenith except when it indi-
cated to the wise men the place where the
Christ Child lay.

I wish that you could have followed with
me from that point the gesture of the Indian
preacher. I wish you could have seen him
stoop as if to enter the lowly manger ; I wish
you could have seen how tenderly he apparently lifted in his arms the Babe of Bethle-
hem ; no word of mine can describe it to you.

He went further than the manger. For a while, I could not trace the clew to that of which he was speaking until suddenly he seemed to be telling of a youth. Some how, though I do not know just how, I caught the idea. Then he held his hand at the height of a boy twelve years of age. I afterwards learned that the Cherokees had no word to indicate "years old," and they expressed it by this peculiar gesture indicating height. Christ was about twelve years old when he went with his parents to Jerusalem and staid to talk with the wise men after his parents started on their homeward march. I have seen many fine actors on the stage, but never yet have I seen one that could be more dramatic than was this Indian preacher when he depicted the mother's terror and consternation on missing her child. Here gesture found expression and voice took important part. When she returned the voice seemed to recede into the distance, to again burst into entreaty, as she pleaded with him to return. As I have said, I knew not a word of Cherokee, but I alone discovered his theme and followed it to the end simply by gesture and facial expression and the modulation of his voice.

My time is nearly up, and yet there is so much to say. When I am talking about my favorite Indians, I want to go on and on forever, no matter how weary my audience becomes. But I must say a word about their schools. I visited their two colleges and some of their common schools. I saw Indians proficient in mathematics, Latin and even Greek. Alas for my pride as a citizen of cultured Ithaca, for one evening one of the learned Indians of the Cherokee Nation came to my room at the Cherokee Hotel, and a dozen or more times he quoted with excellent pronunciation in both Latin and Greek, and I had not the least idea what he was talking about until I returned home and found those quotations in the back part of Webster's Dictionary. After all, Schools in the Cherokee Nation are not unlike those in New York. Even they have college scrapes, but they are more sensible than some we know about in the east. I have been requested to tell one of these Indian College pranks, but it may not be new to you all, for I wrote it for Frank Leslie's Magazine some years ago, and it has several times been reproduced.

VII

You see, old Blindy was an ox that for years was kept around the Seminary buildings for working purposes until he became stone blind, and the managers thought he had out-lived his usefulness, and decreed that he must die to furnish food for the boys' table. When this decree was made the young Cher-okees at once called a Council and were unan-imous, that not a morsel of old Blindy's flesh should pass their lips, and then they inter-ceded for old Blindy's life. But of no avail. So before the time set apart for the execution, the boys by stealth led the ox up the hill. Being blind, he was easily made to follow them up the steep ascent, and at last he was safe on the very top. There in the thicket they concealed and tied him to a sapling, and at once decked him with bark, beads and flowers, and painted his horns with many

colors.   There they fed him until the managers found where old Blindy was and how he
got there, and the boys were ordered to take
him back again.   This they did, escorting him
down to the seminary door in solemn procession.   When there, they tied the rope which
was around old Blindy's neck to the bell pull,
and by the shaking of his head, he summoned
to the door his would-be executioner.   Again
the boys interceded for old Blindy's life, and
when the managers saw their earnest desire
and looked on old Blindy in his gay trimmings
the request was granted, and old Blindy was
permitted to await the approach of a natural
death, which came some years after.

There are 999 things more which I might
tell you about, such as my reception in the
Cherokee Council House, where the Chief in
due form bade me welcome, and a member of
his Council went home and donned in my
honor a swallow tailed dress coat which was
ornamented with enormous brass buttons.   I
went bravely through the informal introduction
to twenty or more Cherokee Senators, and
fifty or more Cherokee Assemblymen, but
when this was over and a score of Cherokee

young ladies, some of them dressed quite fashionably in silks, were presented to me I just wilted. I tell you my friends it is very surprising and embarrassing to a bashful young man from civilization where it is generally supposed that Indians are simply barbarians, to be suddenly confronted by silk dressed Indian belles, some of whom were as graceful as if they had graduated from a metropolitan dancing academy. Some one has asked me to speak of their social life. I attended what I call a high tea in the Cherokee Nation. I went at the special request of a Cherokee maiden. She promised to do all the cooking and I assure you the supper was fine. I wish some of our white girls could cook as well. It was a formal affair and gotten up after the native customs. When a Cherokee Indian starts in life, he begins according to his means. He builds first a hut of one room. If he improves financially, he adds another and so on seldom uniting the rooms. So, when you are in the parlor you must go out of doors to get into the dining or sleeping rooms. When I reached the cabin at the appointed time, no one was visible except the old Indian who was chopping wood. He said "howdy" and pointed to the empty reception room, which we entered, while he kept on chopping wood. A half hour after, the old lady looked into the room and said "howdy," and left at once. About half an hour after, our fair Indian hostess came and showed us to the dining room; we went out of doors to get there. Myself and friend sat at the table, which was up to our chins; the old man continued to chop wood outside; the old woman sat in the corner of the room on a very low stool; the fair Indian girl stood directly behind us, and the feast went merrily on. When our menu was finished. myself and friend went back to the parlor; and the old man left his wood pile, the old woman her stool and with the girl they all sat down and continued the feast where we left off, and we waited for them to get through. This was their way of showing honor to guests. The evening was pleasantly passed by us all together around a roaring fire which was kept burning in a big fire place. All were social except the old Indian, he was painfully embarrassed; whenever he spoke during the evening, he at once left the room and went to the wood pile and brought in a small log of wood. After the big fire place was full, he stacked it up on one side of the cabin until before I left at ten o'clock he had it piled about five feet high. Each log of wood represented a remark by the Indian.

Perhaps you would not think it, but I once stood on a gallows.—a gallows on which twelve bad Indians had been executed. I can assure you it is a peculiar sensation one has, while standing on the gallows on which twelve Indians have been hung, and have the hangman of six of them close beside you. I just mention these facts because the papers of late have been full about an Indian, who was to be shot,* that was given his liberty until the time of execution and he came back on time. I have heard people doubt this story, but I do not. The Cherokee hangman told me several instances of this kind, and if the condemned gets a little late by saying good-

---

*The Cherokees execute their murderers by hanging, the Choctaws shoot whom they condemn to death.

bye at home the preparations for the hanging
go merrily on.   He is sure to be there.   The
hangman told me he never had known an Indian, who was sentenced to death and was allowed to go home to see his people, that
failed to return at the appointed time, and he
never saw evidence of fear on the gallows.

VIII.

*"Howdy!"

The speaker was an Indian, whom I one day met as I was travelling upon the half-road and half-trail that marked one of the lonesome prairies of the Cherokee nation.

The Indian wore a semi-civilized dress, the barbaric epoch being represented by the buckskin trousers, with fringed stripes of fine-cut hide to ornament each leg. In marked contrast with the buckskin breeches was his white vest,—or the one which might have been white when he started upon his journey over the dusty prairie trail.

His coat was before him on the saddle;

---

*This chapter is taken from the "Green Bag," a law magazine published in Boston, the subject matter being the author's notes on Cherokee laws and courts which he made while in the Cherokee Nation.

beneath his white vest he wore a red shirt; a black tie coiled beneath the overlapping shirt-collar, and was fastened in a sailor-knot in front.

Simultaneously with his exclamation of "Howdy!" he emphatically drew his bridle, and his little Cherokee pony stopped short; and bringing mine to a standstill, we began to size each other up as strangers do when they meet alone on the prairie.

"You are a friend of the Cherokees," he said; "you wrote the life of our greatest man."

His remark was at the same time an affirmation and interrogation. He noticed my look of admission and surprise, and said, "I heard that you were over there,"—pointing toward Tahlequah, the Cherokee capital. "But few people come to this nation unless we know who they are, and what they are here for. It is well that it is so, if they are white men."

Glancing at his well-filled haversack, which hung at his pony's side, I noticed several leather-covered books protruding from its open top. Desiring to show penetrative faculties equal to the Indian's, I said, both interrogatively and affirmatively, "Colporteur?"

Whether he knew what I meant or not, I do not know; but he appeared pleased that I had noticed his books. He laughed, and in a good-natured way, tapping his haversack with his finger, he said,—

"Heap law there!"

"Then you are a lawyer," I said.

I had been previously informed concerning these travelling Indian lawyers, and was not surprised to receive his profound bow of assent.

Rev. A. N. Chamberlain, a lifelong resident, teacher, missionary, also interpreter in the Cherokee country, had said to me, "I presume that there is no people anywhere better informed than the non-English speaking Cherokees are in regard to their laws, and their treaties with the United States."

I had here an English-speaking Cherokee armed and equipped with his law library, and I resolved to interview him.

The mid-day sun was scorching the prairie, and there was no convenient shade-tree; but it was only the work of an instant for the Indian lawyer to unroll his blanket, in which were four sticks, some over three feet long.

Having dismounted, he stuck these sticks in the ground, and threw the blanket over them; and into the shade of this hastily improvised sun-umbrella, or wickeyup, he invited me, and at my request, while the incense of pure "havanas," which I furnished, was wafted upward, he displayed his law library,—the code of the Cherokee nation.

An ancient-looking book, printed in English, was a compilation of the laws which were adopted by the Cherokee Council at various periods previous to 1852. It surprised me, and may be surprising to others to know, that the compilation occupied nearly two hundred and fifty pages; and many of the laws were passed by their Council before the Cherokees took their long, sad journey from Georgia to the land which they now occupy. The first of the compiled laws was one dated 1808, concerning horse-stealing,—the convicted thief to be punished with one hundred lashes on the bare back.

"The Cherokee tradition concerning the reception of their first law is not unlike that of your own people," said the lawyer.

"Some time after the red man entered the

wilderness, they came to a very high mountain, and their God came down upon the
mountain, and their leader went up and con-
versed with God,—or, rather, as their fathers
said, with the son of God. They supposed,
therefore, that God had a son, as it was said
to be the son of God that came down on the
mountain; and the top of the mountain was
bright like the sun. There God gave the
leader a law, written on a smooth stone. The
reason of this being written on stone was as
follows :—

"God gave our first parents a law to be
handed down to posterity ; but when the language was destroyed, and men began to quar-
rel and kill each other. they forgot this law ;
and therefore God wrote his law on stone,
that it might not be lost. Their leader also
received other instructions from God, which
he wrote in a book made of skins."

And so it happened that a long time before
the Cherokees reached the country which they
now occupy, they had a full code of laws.

They had striven to imitate the whites in
the management of their affairs, and their
Councils were well conducted. In 1810 the

Council abolished clans, and unanimously passed an act of oblivion for all lives for which they had been indebted one to another. In 1820 the nation was reorganized, and, by a resolve of its National Council, divided into eight districts, each of which had the privilege of sending four members to their legislature. Some of their principal laws and regulations : A prohibition of spirituous liquor to be brought into the nation by white men.   If a white man took a Cherokee wife, he must marry her according to their laws ; but her property was not affected by such union. No man was allowed but one wife.   A judge, sheriff, and two deputies were allowed each district.   Embezzlement, intercepting and opening sealed letters, were punished by a fine of a hundred dollars, and one hundred lashes on the bare back. They had a statute of limitations, which, however, did not affect notes.   A will was valid if found, on the decease of its maker, to have been written by him, and witnessed by two creditable persons.   A man leaving no will, all his children shared equal, and his wife as one of them; if he left no children, then the widow had a fourth part of all the property, the other three-fourths going to his nearest relatives. Even before the division of the nation into districts, and the appointment of a judge, marshal, sheriffs, and deputies, there was an organized company of light horse, which executed the orders of the chief, searched out offenders, and brought them to justice. It was a fundamental law of the Cherokees that no land should be sold to the white people without the authority of a majority of the nation. Transgressors of this law were punished with death.

The Cherokee lawyer now replaced the old law-book—which, by the way, was printed wholly in English—carefully in his haversack, and took out two more volumes. They were handsomely printed, bound in leather, and one was printed in English, the other in the Cherokee language, and in the alphabet that Sequo-yah, one of the learned members of their tribe, had given them over half a century ago.

"These are our latest compilations," said the Indian lawyer, with a proud manner, opening the covers of the book and turning over the pages.

"In spite of what the whites say about us,

you can see that we are far from being a lawless people, and possibly we can give the white men a point or two on the enforcement of law ourselves." By Cherokee law, every killing of a human being, without the authority of law, by stabbing, shooting, poisoning, or other means, is either murder or manslaughter, in the first, second, or third degree, according to the intention of the person perpetrating the act, and the facts and circumstances connected with each act. If the killing is done intentionally or with premeditated design, the convicted person must suffer death by hanging; if done without design to effect death, or by culpable negligence, the term of imprisonment is not less than two years. Abortionists are imprisoned for not less than two or more than ten years; seconds and medical advisers in prize-fights, where death occurs, are deemed guilty of manslaughter. Rape is punished by imprisonment from ten to twenty-five years, and the ravishment of female children is punished by hanging. From five to fifteen years is the imprisonment for arson; and if death results from the fire, death is the prospective fate of the one convicted.

"Marriage and divorce are now subject to law with as much strictness as in the States. No marriage can be contracted while either of the parties has a husband or wife living, or between persons of a kin nearer than first cousins ; and a heavy penalty is inflicted on any who join minors in marriage without the consent of their parents. Divorces are regulated by law, and are adjudged for adultery, imprisonment for three years, for wilful desertion or neglect for one year, for extreme cruelty or habitual drunkenness. The Cherokees as a people have always favored temperance, and have an effective prohibitory law on the statutes. The United States law lays a penalty on any white man or Indian who brings liquor across the line of the Territory, for any purpose whatever. The Cherokee laws lay a penalty upon the sale of any liquor after it is brought into the country.

"So," said the lawyer, "you see that the Cherokees are a law-abiding people; and their laws must certainly be looked upon with interest and respect by all civilized nations of the world."

"How about the enforcement of law?" I queried.

"The judiciary system is divided into Supreme, Circuit, and District Courts. The Supreme Court consists of three judges, one of whom is selected by a joint vote of the National Council as Chief-Justice.

"The power of the Supreme Court is about the same as the power of a similar body in the States,—the decision made has the force of law. The judges have and exercise exclusive criminal jurisdiction in all cases of manslaughter, and in all cases involving punishment of death; this court also has exclusive jurisdiction of all cases instituted to contest an election held by the people, and brought before it as provided by law; they have power to award judgments, order decrees, and to issue such writs and processes as they may find necessary to carry into full effect the power vested in them by law. There are three judicial circuits,—the Northern, Middle, and Southern; and one judge is elected for each circuit. The circuit courts have jurisdiction in all criminal cases, except those of manslaughter, and cases involving directly or indirectly a sum exceeding one hundred dollars, and all civil suits in which the title to real estate or the right to the occupancy of any portion of the common domain shall be at issue, exceeding one hundred dollars. There is also a district court for each district, for trying of all criminal cases, whether felonies or misdemeanors, involving the sum of one hundred dollars or less."

"Then you have a jury system?" I said.

"Yes; but no man is allowed as a juror who is under twenty-one years of age, nor any person who may be under punishment for misdemeanor; and no member of the legislative or any commissioned officer of the nation, officiating clergyman, physician, lawyer, public ferryman, school-teacher, or one older than sixty-five years, is compelled to serve as juror or as guard. Five persons constitute a jury in the trial of all civil suits, any three of whom may render a verdict. In case of murder, twelve jurymen are required; but in all other cases the jury consists of nine persons; and no verdict is rendered in any criminal case without the consent of the whole jury. The grand jurors are selected with especial care from the best and most intellectual men in the nation. The term of service is for one year unless discharged.   Five men are summoned from each district for this purpose.

"I am on my way to court now," said the lawyer; "will you go with me?"   And consenting, I rode back with him to the court house.

The case on trial was something like this :—

A white man had married a Cherokee woman, and therefore was the possessor of a farm ; and for a period of three days had employed, without permit of the court, a white boy.   The warrant set forth that "thereby the peace and dignity of the Cherokee nation had been damaged to the extent of seventy-five dollars."

No citizen of the United States is permitted to labor in the Cherokee nation without a permit, which is issued by the district clerk, and which shows the name of the employer and employee, the length of time to be employed, and the occupation to be followed.   For such permit the employer pays in advance one dollar per month to the clerk; but no permit is given for a longer time than a year.   The person "permitted" is obliged to subscribe to the following oath, to wit :—

"I do solemnly swear [or affirm] that I am a citizen of the United States [or a foreigner]; that it is not on account of any criminal offence against the laws of the same that I have come to seek employment in this nation ; that within ten (10) days after the expiration of my permit, unless the same shall be renewed, I will remove without the limits of this nation."

It was for the violation of the permit law that the employer was under arrest. At an early hour Cherokees of all grades had assembled in the vicinity of the court-house. The sheriff soon came to the door, and summoned his jury. Looking over the crowd, with stentorian voice he shouted,—

"Ho-ho-o-o-o-o, Hog Catcher ! Ho-ho-o-o-o-o, Six Killer ! Ho-ho-o-o-o-o you, Coming Deer ! Ho-ho-o-o-o-o you, Walking Stick ! Ho-ho-o-o-o-o you, Kingfisher ! Ho-ho-o-o-o-o you, Muskrat !" and his jury was complete.

I am not absolutely sure that I have recorded the names of this particular jury correctly ; some of these names were summoned, and the other names are frequently met with, and their owners find their way from time to time into the jury seats.

This assemblage was by far the most novel of any that I saw in the nation. Men, women, and children sat around the stove, or gathered in little groups about the oak-grove that surrounded the court-house. Most all were smoking, and all were in their every-day dress. The jurymen, six in number, had gathered behind the rail that separated the jury seats, counsel seats, and judge's table from the gaping crowd outside.

The gate leading behind the rail was closed as the jurymen took their seats; but while the court was in session, any one wishing to speak to the lawyers and judge usually straddled over the rail in preference to opening the gate. The jurymen could all speak English save one; an interpreter was sworn in for his benefit, and all the evidence was given twice, —first in English, and then in Cherokee. As the case proceeded, and the evidence grew more complicated, the jury dropped into apparently deep meditation. Finally one drew out a long pipe, filled it with tobacco, and commenced to smoke. Another and another of the jurymen followed with a pipe. The interested audience outside the bars also lit their pipes, and at length the judge, five of the jurymen, and nearly the whole audience were smoking.

To show the inconsistency of their etiquette, I mention that while all were thus smoking, in order to protect myself from a draught of air, as I sat by a window, I put on my travelling-cap. Had I been in a more dignified court in the States, I should not have done so; but in this assemblage blue with the smoke of tobacco, I forgot myself, and in a few minutes was brought to grief by being touched lightly on the shoulder by one in authority, who also had a pipe in his mouth, who said,—

"Your pardon, sir; but it is not customary in our nation to wear one's hat in the presence of the judge."

Notwithstanding this reproof, I listened to the arguments of the lawyers with pleasure. They were well posted in regard to their laws, and handled their respective sides with shrewdness. The Cherokee lawyers displayed a marked logical penetration into the meaning and intent of the laws, and a weak place in a witness's testimony was quickly detected; and he was most unmercifully handled when the lawyer summed up the case.

IX.

One beautiful morning some years ago, behold a grand procession moving down the main street of the Cherokee capital. First two big dogs,—of which figuratively speaking the Cherokee nation has thousands,—led the way, just as soberly as would two city policemen on a like occasion. Next was an Indian pony on which sat a half-breed Indian dressed in cowboy's hat, which had an ornament of a feather pulled from a rooster's tail. He wore also a brown jacket, and trousers of same color and had a big six shooter protruding from a cartridge belt. Next came two vicious, stately, long eared mules, followed by a wagon of doubtful build, the dasher of which had long since been ruined by the viciousness of mulish heels, and in this wagon and behind these mules in pomp and state sat the Cherokee Chief and he who speaks to you this evening. All the people seemed to be on the streets drawn up in line. Down by the Cherokee hotels, the stores and the great Council House we went out into the beautiful suburbs to a trail down which years ago, moved a far more famous expedition than was our own, for it was on this other bright morning in 1840, that there passed down this trail one of the most peculiar expeditions in search of knowledge that this world has ever known. First and foremost in that company was that Indian Se-quo-yah, who had invented the alphabet that had so helped in enlightening and christianizing his people.* He had conceived a new idea, that of forming an alphabet by which all Indians could speak and read a common language and thus better

---

*The author has a personal letter from Rev. A. N. Chamberlin, life-long missionary and official interpreter for the Cherokee Nation in which he writes :—

"As to the amount of good Se-quo-yah's alphabet has done our people it is beyond estimation. At least ten thousand people read today who could not were it not for Se-quo-yah's alphabet. Untold thousands since 1827 have been led through it to Jesus.

work together for the upbuilding of the Indian race. To do this he thought to study the language of all western tribes and hence it was that in 1840 he started as I have said on the most wonderful expedition for the search of knowledge that this world has ever known. He started with a Cherokee boy, two oxen and a rude Indian cart. Two years did that wonderful knowledge crusade move from tribe to tribe,—but, alas Se-quo-yah died with his task unfinished—before the culmination of his grand conception—a conception so great, that no human being though a white man, ever conceived the like before—that of forming a more wonderful alphabet, one that would enable all Indian tribes of North America to read and speak the common language, that would enable them to unite in forming a grand confederacy for the purpose of defense, for the mutual preservation from the encroachments of the white men and their lasting perpetuation in the land deeded to the Indians by Almighty God.

On my return to the Council House I was taken into the room devoted to the use of the Board of Education, and I noted a marble bust over the president's seat, and says I, what white man is this that the Cherokees thus honor in marble. And then one Cherokee with face glowing with enthusiasm such as only National pride can give said : "This is no white man, this is Se-quo-yah, the Cherokee, a pale face preserved in marble the memory of the Father of his Country—the Cherokee in the same way honors the Father of Learning to his people and that bust is a token of gratitude, which was carved at the order of the Cherokee Council. Down in the Senate room of the Cherokee Capitol, the Cherokee Senate did me a special honor, they passed a resolution of thanks for the book I had written, which was signed by the principal Chief and others in authority, thanks as the document read for my interest in showing to the world that there could be something good and even great in the American Indian. This document was sealed with the seal of the Nation and it is said was the first document of the kind ever given by the red race to a white man.

X

My journey was a mixture of rain, sunshine and tornadoes. "What a charming morning!" I exclaimed to my Creek host, the proprietor of a log cabin near Okmulgee, where I had been to see the handsome Council-house of the Creeks, which was fully fifty miles from the chief's home. "What a contrast it was to the raging elements of a few hours ago!" I continued, thinking of the storm of the evening previous, when the scattering clouds rolled themselves into a darker ball, and by thus coming into closer contact had fretted themselves into fury, and then tore across the country in pitiless force. Although I did not know it then, that storm, as raged in the northward, had twisted down huge trees, plowed wide furrows in thick forests, and had sent the debris of scores of frail homes of a Western village flying through the air as easily as thistledown is carried on the September breeze. But the morning was indeed charming, and yet the storm had in no way cooled the air. A slight haze now hung over the forest, which fringed a stream far over the prairie. The diamond drops sparkled in the bosom of many variegated and gaudy flowers. Even while I looked, the haze suddenly lifted from the far-off trees; the darker clouds turned first yellow, and then red, the colors finally fading until they melted away, leaving the sky an azure blue.

"It will be some time before there will be another storm," I remarked to my Creek host, who had by this time put on his wide-rimmed white hat, having on it a band of down, ornamented with three long feathers of a rooster's tail.

"May rain a heap more soon; no tell; pretty much may; heap hot—look out," replied my host.

The Creek's surmises were right, for, as late that afternoon I rode across the prairie to a small station to board a train for a little village further down on the Missouri Pacific, I saw once more clouds gathering in the West.

Before the train arrived they had rolled themselves up into a mountain-heap of blackness.
Once the setting sun lit up the cloud-bank,
and it resembled a spacious castle made of
jasper and precious stones.

"Another shower to the eastward—look
out!" said a fellow loiterer at the station, as
he noted the lightning playing on a similar
cloud-bank in that direction. Before I stepped
into the train I noticed that the cloud in the
west had started as if in chase after the one
in the east. Then the lightning began to be
so sharp and vivid that the whole prairie for
miles in every direction was a blaze of electric
light, and each tree, shrub, leaf, flower and
spear of grass was covered with the glow of
silver. The lightning came in sheets at first,
but soon a shower of flame began falling from
the heavens. It was not a storm where now
and then streaks of zigzag, forked lightning
appeared to unite earth and heaven, but it
was more as if the million raindrops had been
converted into streams of liquid fire, for soon
the whole space between earth and heaven
was ablaze with celestial rockets. Nearer and
nearer, faster and faster. like the feet of a

million race horses, came down upon us this battery of electric fire; the roar of the thunder was tremendous, causing the train to tremble as it rushed along the prairie. Suddenly there was a flash so blinding that it seemed as if all the streams of falling fire had blended into one. The deafening cannonade that followed was as if the earth was rent in twain. The storm then struck the cars. Every lamp went out, and a billow of water, like that of a tempestuous sea, rolled over us. It found its way through cracks and crevices of the cars, and came in large quantities down from the ventilators overhead. For a few moments we were in a darkness that could be felt, and the cars swayed to and fro like a boat on the boiling ocean. That was the heaviest part of the storm. In a few moments it had rolled to the eastward, and in a few minutes more the moon came out and painted the clouds with a silvery hue, and the great chariot of fire rolled away in the far distance.

XI

When the war of the rebellion broke out, the Cherokees were compelled to fight the white man's battles, and again was the population quartered by death. Terrible is the story of the Cherokees' fate in the Civil War. I have listened to this tale of woe from the lips of many a Cherokee man, and gray headed Indian women have told me of the suffering then, and, as they spoke, their eyes filled with tears while they for a few moments recalled those agonizing hours. I have already told you how in their first terrible march from Georgia and Tennessee in 1838, they suffered from excessive heat, but in their flight for safety in 1862 they suffered from most bitter cold. Their horses, their beds and bedding and wearing apparel were taken away. In the battle and the pursuit which was long and fierce and bloody, horses and

Indians froze to death. The Confederates on every hand murdered and robbed the loyal Cherokees. And the Cherokees abandoned every thing and fled to the mountains where they remained during the winter, exposed in their destitute condition to all the inclemencies of the season. The Cherokees first fought on the side of the South, being told by the Southern Emissaries that the South was the successor of the United States, but they soon learned their mistake.

Those disloyal Indians under the influence of the Southern Emissaries were organized into "Blue Lodges" and "Knights of the Golden Circle," while the loyal masses by a spontaneous movement, organized themselves into a loyal league known as the "Ketoowah" society. The "Ketoowah" societies had for a primary object to resist encroachments on native rights, and to preserve according to an early treaty the integrity and peace of the Cherokee Nation, but it finally united in working for the abolishment of slavery, and by its means a large majority of the Cherokees became at length firmly grounded in their fidelity to the United States Government. And when one day the Confederate forces in revenge swept through the Cherokee Nation and left the stars and bars, the flag of secession, floating from a staff near the Cherokee capitol, a Cherokee woman, true to the Union, tore it down and ran up the Star Spangled banner, which never came down again.

For many years the Cherokees were slaveholders and there were many slaves in the Cherokee Nation. When the war was over and the remnant of the Cherokee people returned to their devastated homes, the Cherokee slaveholders were the first to free their slaves, and it was done by an act of the Cherokee Council before any Southern state obeyed the emancipation proclamation of Abraham Lincoln.*

---

*On the 21st of August, 1861, the Cherokees, finding themselves at the mercy of the Confederate forces and practically left to their fate by the Federal Government, met in convention at Tahlequah and resolved to make a treaty of peace with the Confederate authorities ; but on February 18, 1863, finding themselves no longer constrained by superior force, a national council was held at Cowskin Prairie, where the treaty was denounced as null and void, any office held by a disloyal Chero-

But how sad was the return of the Cherokees. Their public buildings had been devastated, their little libraries were destroyed, their well preserved archives and much of their written history were forever lost. Even the sacred silver pipe given to the Cherokees

---

kee was declared vacant, and, more remarkable still, an act was passed abolishing slavery in the Cherokee Nation. Through the kindness of the chief, I have been permitted to copy an act from the records :

AN ACT EMANCIPATING THE SLAVE IN THE CHEROKEE NATION.

Be it enacted by the National Council : That all negro and other slaves within the lands of the Cherokee Nation be and they are hereby emancipated from slavery, and any person or persons who may have been held in slavery *are hereby declared to be forever free.*

Be it further enacted, That this act shall go into effect on the twenty-fifth (25th) day of June, 1863. And any person who, after the said 25th day of June, 1863, shall offend against the provisions of this act, by enslaving or holding any person in slavery within the limits of the Cherokee Nation, he or she so offending shall, on conviction thereof before any of the Courts of this nation having jurisdiction of the case, forfeit and pay for each offense a sum not less than one thousand ($1000) dollars, or more than five thousand ($5000) dollars, at the discretion of the Court.

Two-thirds of said fine shall be paid in the National Treasury, and one-third shall be paid, in

by George Washington was stolen. Schools
and churches were broken up, and, said Chief
Ross, "there was not a footprint of cattle or
swine in any part of the Cherokee Nation."
For during the conflict the Cherokees were
robbed by their enemies of one-fourth of all
they had and their reputed friends did not
hesitate to take all the rest.

---

equal sums, to the Solicitor and the sheriff of the
District in which the offense shall have been committed. And it is hereby made the duty of the
Solicitors of the several Districts to see that this
law is duly enforced. But in case any Solicitor
shall neglect or fail to discharge his duties herein,
and shall be convicted thereof, he shall be deposed
from his office, and shall hereafter be ineligible to
hold any office of trust or honor in this nation.

The Acting Principal Chief is hereby required to
give due notice of this act.

Be it further enacted, That all laws and parts of
laws conflicting with the provisions of this act are
hereby repealed.

COWSKIN PRAIRIE, C. N.
Feb. 21st, 1863.

J. B. JONES,
Clerk National Com.
Concurred in Council.

LEWIS DOWNING,
Pres. pro tem.
School Com.

SPRING FROG,
Speaker of Council.

Approved Feb. 21st, 1863.

THOS. PEGG,
Acting Principal Chief.

XII.

Are Indians human beings? They are intensely so. They have a love of home, as much as have we who call ourselves civilized ; they love their kindred just as we love ours. From earliest history they have most tenderly cared for their orphan children. When their wigwam villages were first visited by the white men, in the very center of their camp could always be found a principal wigwam in which the old dames of the Cherokee people tenderly cared for the little orphans. The Cherokees have no wigwams today, but cabins and some elegant residences. Their orphan children are no longer cared for in a center wigwam, but they have an elegant orphan asylum, where the fatherless of the Cherokees get a liberal education. They have a fine insane asylum, a prison, and a council house that cost them at least $22,000. There are

Masonic Lodges in the Cherokee lands, and I was informed that the Cherokees made excellent members.

As the multiplicity of scenes of Indian travel pass before me in panoramic array there are some reminiscent only in name for their memory is constant—a haunt if you choose so to call it. I see them in the morning sunshine, I see them as the sun shines at the zenith, or in the golden twilight hour, or in my dreams in the blackness of the night. I see so often those lonely graves on the prairies, where some white man or white woman seeking homes in the far West had buried by the wayside, some father, mother, husband, wife or child, and gone on leaving these graves—but not without anguish, to the care only of the great black winged vultures, which seemed to me too often to be the only official sextons in that western wilderness.

But friends, there were four thousand of these lonely graves made by the wayside, or by pathless trails, just sixty years ago, due to white men's injustice to the Indians. And the survivors, being human. mourned their dead with as keen an anguish as if they too were white men. The lonely graves in the wilderness! I came across one miles away from human habitations,—new it was—it had been hollowed out only by some near friend, who had erected upon it a cross of rude sticks and twined about it a wreath of prairie grass, and then gone on leaving this mound behind him. *Last year, my friends, I took you to the grave of Samuel A. Worcester and pointed out the tree that had grown from his grave, and which had taken unto itself all that was mortal of that good old missionary. I pointed out a tree that had taken the form of a hand, the index finger of which seemed to be pointing heavenward. But, ladies, I was not unmindful that there were other lonely graves in the wilderness,—graves not of men, but of women, brave, true-hearted women, who years ago had homes in the East, beautiful and as full of comforts as our own homes are today. They were surrounded by kindred and friends, but yet they left these homes, kindred and all, and went into the pathless wilderness to carry the Gospel to the redmen : and faithfully they

---

*See Cherokee Bible page 32.

labored; cheerfully they bore deprivations; and finally died in the wilderness, but with the blessed assurance that their labor had been abundantly blessed. My friends, when we feel it a hardship to drop a penny or a nickel into the contribution box to aid the missionaries, let us stop and rest a minute; yes, two minutes if it is necessary, and think of these lonely graves and what the life record of those who lie buried there mean to us and to civilization. I was glad to see that those graves of noble Christian missionaries though uncared for by human hand, yet were cared for by the hand of Nature. Some little birds perhaps or some autumnal zephyr had scattered the seeds of the wild white star flowers that there were blooming. I was so glad to see the white star flower blooming there for it seemed so synonymous of the pure lives of those that had been there laid to rest. Yes, I was glad that they were the white star flowers —for it has been said the stars of heaven are as the flowers of earth,—but it seemed to me that those flowers of earth, those faithful missionary women, had become as it were the Brightest Stars of Heaven.

www.ingramcontent.com/pod-product-compliance
Lightning Source LLC
Chambersburg PA
CBHW020326090426
42735CB00009B/1420